# STEVE BAILEY'S ROCK BASS

## The Ultimate Rock Bass Workout

## Contents

**Photography by Margaret Ford and Leeann Bailey**

Alfred Publishing Co., Inc.
16320 Roscoe Blvd., Suite 100
P.O. Box 10003
Van Nuys, CA 91410-0003
alfred.com

ISBN-10: 0-7390-4080-4 (Book & CD)
ISBN-13: 978-0-7390-4080-5 (Book & CD)

# Introduction

Possibly, at this moment, in a dark recording studio somewhere in Los Angeles, sits an engineer, a producer, and a bass player. They are putting the finishing touches to the bass line of what might be the next platinum single from a major rock and roll band. The throbbing pulse of an eighth-note bass groove pushes the chorus into overdrive as the guitar screams over the lead and background vocals. Thirty seconds later the producer pushes the stop button on the remote control box, the red lights go off and the tape grinds to a halt. "We'll be faded out by this point—incredible job—you did it again! Let's go celebrate."

What's wrong with this picture?

The bassist with the producer is not the bassist whose name and picture appears on the CD jacket. He's not the bassist who spent countless hours rehearsing and recording the basic tracks for this record. The bassist who "saved this song" is not the one who will be hurt, humiliated, and quite unhappy to find out the producer brought in somebody else to ghost his tracks. Sounds like a drag, doesn't it? The producer is not the "bad guy." His ultimate responsibility is to "produce" a great record and present it to the record company. He can't do that if one of the main ingredients (the bass line) has fret buzz, noise, bad timing, bad tone, or any combination of the above!

Having been the "hired gun" brought in by the producer more times than I care to remember, I decided to put on paper the techniques and concepts that could eventually put me out of the "hired gun" business. If the principles in these pages are adhered to and practiced, the odds are much greater that you—the bassist in the band—will emerge from the studio (as well as the stage) confident that your artistry will be heard by millions.

The basic concepts for this book were initially conceived as curriculum for Rock Bass class at the Bass Institute of Technology in Hollywood, California.

# About the Book

1. Most units are arranged with the "meat" of the lesson first, including numerous exercises. This material is followed by "Technique Builders," a series of exercises designed to build skillful technique. Next comes the "Lick of the Week," an etude of high technical demand, the essence of which is derived from the previous lesson material.

2. All exercises should be practiced with a metronome or a solid drum machine pattern.

3. The Technique Builders should be reviewed frequently, and tempos should be increased when all transitions are smooth and consistent. (Keep a log of your progress and set weekly goals.)

4. As you will notice, there is an emphasis on getting the most out of each practice session. Condition your brain and hands to work together. For example, try to be aware of your left-hand fingering, right-hand alternation and consistency, and your time feel. To combine all three is a major accomplishment, but with practice and concentration, you will get more out of a one-hour practice session than you ever imagined.

5. If you don't read music notation, start relating the TAB notes to what is written above. Reading music will only open more doors for you.

# Unit 1:
## Right-Hand Alternation (Picking)

Whether you use a one-, two-, or even a three-finger right-hand technique, there is one basic concept for success: proper balance of evenness, consistency, and control. Whether you use a two- or three-finger technique, each attack should sound the same—like one finger.

Without consistent, even attack, your eighth and sixteenth notes won't provide that smooth, solid "floor" upon which harmony and melody should firmly sit. Without consistency, you (along with the drummer) won't be able to sustain that evenness throughout the length of a verse, much less an entire song. Without control over the individual fingers, accents, nuances, and rhythmic embellishments will not be executed accurately; subsequently, your evenness and consistency will suffer (along with your employment consistency). Let the music and your instincts be your guide.

### Single-Note Studies for the Right Hand

The following exercises will help make your journey through this book, as well as your career, a little more "in the pocket." Both two- and three-finger techniques will be addressed. Right-hand fingerings are labeled as follows:

> *i* = index finger
>
> *m* = middle finger
>
> *r* = ring finger

These exercises must be practiced extremely slowly to ensure proper development of the basic concept. Starting with even attack, then consistency, and finally control, these exercises should give you a very solid, basic alternation technique. Only time and practice will integrate these concepts into your everyday playing. Rules are made to be broken, so deviations from these techniques (raking, breaking sequence) may be necessary to facilitate certain passages (wide intervals, string crossing, etc.). Let your instincts be your guide.

Repeat each exercise many times and speed up *slowly*! Stress *evenness* and *consistency*!

### Two-Finger Technique

#### Example 1

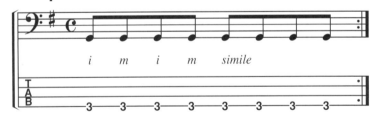

#### Example 2

**Example 3**

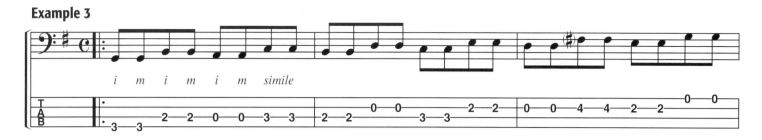

## Three-Finger Technique

My three-finger technique is based on *i-m-r-m* alternation. This makes sixteenth-note passages simple, but requires *extreme* dedication and discipline to master.

Practice all your scales and arpeggios using this right-hand fingering.

**Example 4**    **Example 5**

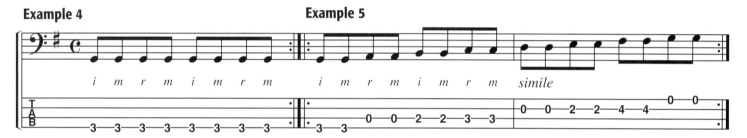

# Control Exercises

Hopefully, you are applying the previous right-hand exercises to all the scales and patterns that you already know (as well as to all the exercises in this book).

## Two-Finger Technique

The following are more difficult exercises emphasizing control. Pay particular attention to the accent markings. Use your imagination, and make up variations on each of these exercises.

**Example 6**

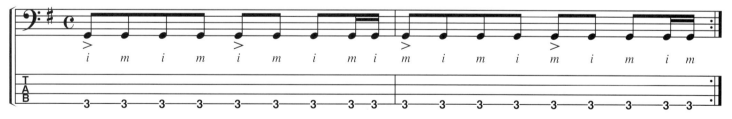

**Example 7
(Shuffle feel)**

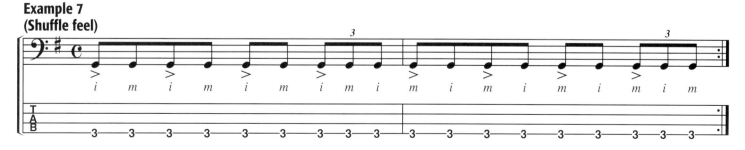

**Example 8**

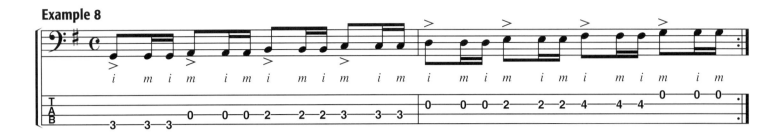

**Example 9**

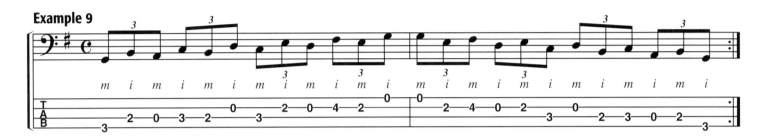

## Three-Finger Technique

When first learning three-finger right-hand technique, I soon realized that I would have to achieve extremely even control over all three fingers, both collectively and individually. These basic exercises will get you started. Expand on these and take your time while incorporating this technique into your playing. Pay attention to accents.

### Three-Finger Exercise 1

Note: These exercises can also be played with a two-finger technique. Make sure to keep your alternation even.

**Three-Finger Exercise 2**
**(Shuffle feel)**

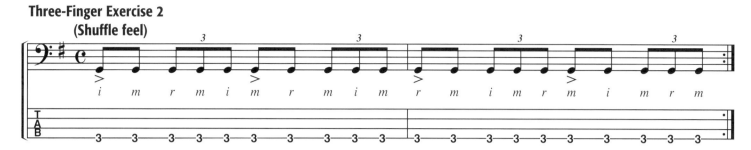

**Three-Finger Exercise 3**

**Three-Finger Exercise 4**

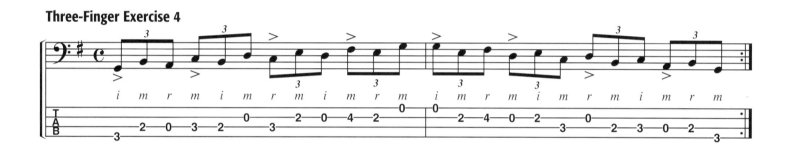

The previous exercises covered the basic fundamentals for good right-hand finger technique. Apply them to all these exercises (be patient) as well as your everyday warm-ups and performances. Don't forget to start at *slow* tempos and to move the metronome up one notch every few days (not before each is mastered at the previous tempo).

A metronome and a pencil are very important for your practice routine; the metronome for obvious reasons, and the pencil so you can write in the tempo and the date over each exercise. This will enable you to monitor your progress. Every time you feel comfortable with a tempo, move the metronome up a notch and mark both the date and tempo. For example:

5/2/07 m.m. 160

5/9/07 m.m. 162

5/29/07 m.m. 164

From the 1950s to the new millennium, there has been one common denominator in all of rock and roll, from Chuck Berry and the Beatles to Led Zeppelin, Van Halen, and Megadeth: the eighth note has been the nucleus of the groove. No matter how we embellish, accent, or displace these eighth notes, if they are not played accurately or "in the pocket," they won't work.

**Exercise 10:** This is a basic eighth-note pattern. Whether you use two- or three-finger right-hand technique, this exercise should sound like it's being played by one finger. All fingers should attack evenly.

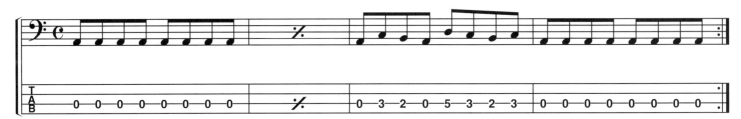

**Exercise 11:** Practice this very slowly and concentrate on evenness. Make sure your string crossing is smooth and concise. Speed up slowly!

**Exercise 12:** As an option, you can use extended fingerings (see Unit 11). Play smoothly and make sure your right-hand alternation is accurate!

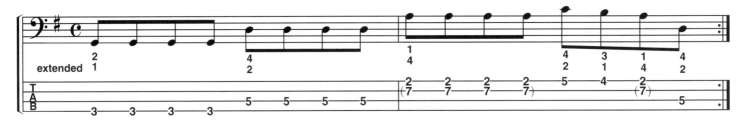

Extended Fingering Exercise 12

**Exercise 13:** This exercise emphasizes right-hand accuracy. Start it slowly and make all notes sound like they were played by one finger. Your right hand is your *pulse*.

## Technique Builders

**Exercise 14:** Set the metronome *very slow* and do this exercise from the beginning to end. These will take a while so please be patient. You must build your stamina slowly. If it hurts, stop, rest, and then start again.

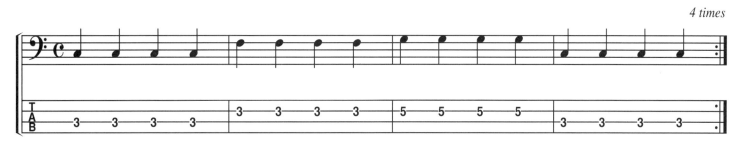

**Variations 1–4:** Use the previous note sequence (C, F, G, C) in the following four variations.

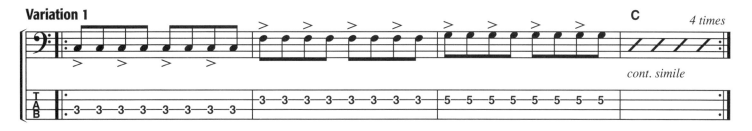

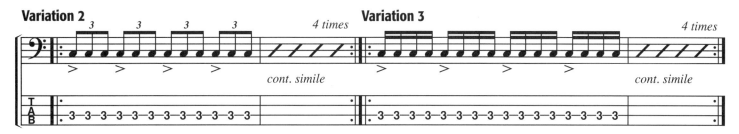

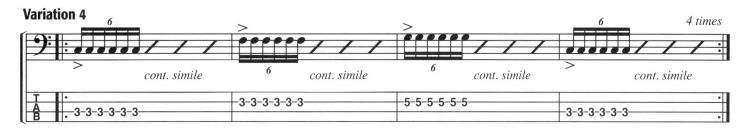

**Exercise 15:** Just when you thought it was over! Try groups of 7, 9, and 11 also. Although you will rarely be asked to play these odd groups, control over them will make easy things a joke, hard things easy, and impossible things possible.

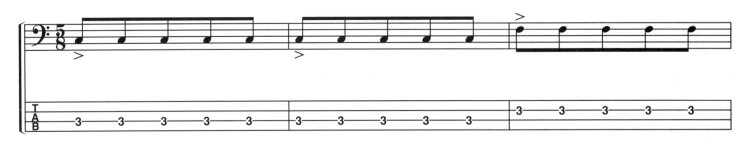

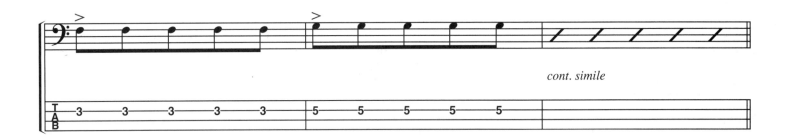

## Lick of the Week

There are many fingering options for this Lick of the Week. Experiment and find the one that works well for your hand size.

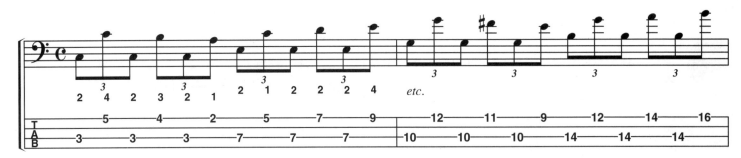

# Unit 2: Eighth-Note Studies

**Exercise 1**: These next exercises should prove very helpful, both for right-hand consistency and for fingerboard knowledge. Practice slowly at first, gradually increasing speed. These are also great for incorporating into a solo.

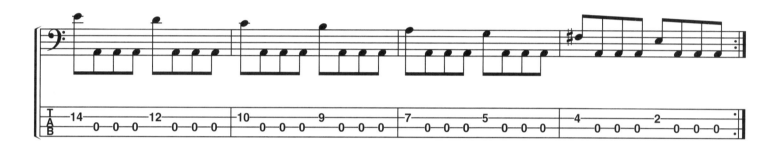

**Exercise 2:** Try to invent different left-hand fingerings. Exercise 2 double-times Exercise 1 and moves the ascending melody from the first note to the second note of the sixteenth-note pattern. Concentrate on right-hand alternation and consistency throughout by using a metronome or some other tempo reference (drum machine, computer). There are many different permutations; for example, changing the bottom note (e.g., to A♭ or G) makes it more difficult.

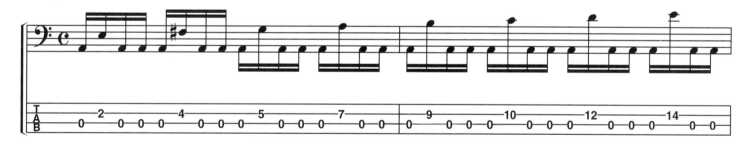

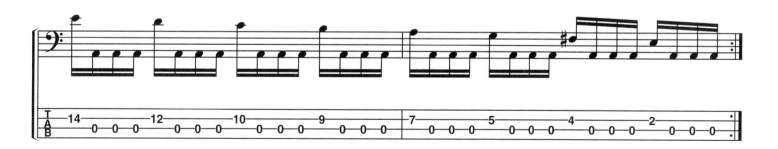

These next five variations continue to displace the ascending melody to various parts of the beat.

## Variations 1–5

### Variation 1

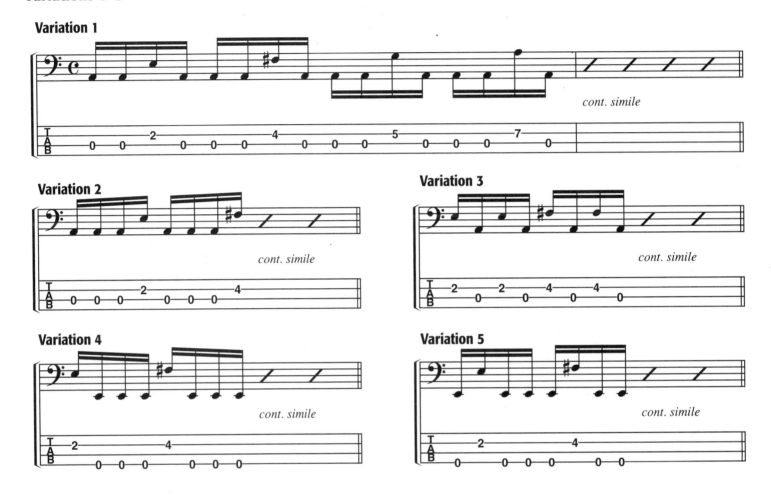

Note: Make sure you play very evenly and "in the pocket." If you have a drum machine, set up syncopated patterns and play your exercises through them.

## Lick of the Week

Try conventional (one-finger-per-fret) fingering as well as extended fingering.

# Hazard Exercises

As the name implies, "Hazard Exercises" can be very straining as well as difficult. If practiced diligently, they will become easy. Once mastered, they serve as excellent warm-up exercises (before gigs, etc.). Please practice these exercises a short time each day. Mastery of these usually take quite some time. Don't give up.

**Hazard 1:** The notes themselves are not difficult; retaining finger position is the "hazard." These are particularly good for third- and fourth-finger independence. Where you see an asterisk(*), keep that finger down on the note until the shift. The asterisk marks the "hazard."

Eventually, you should condition yourself to where it's possible to play the entire length of the *neck*! Hazard Exercises 2–5 coming later.

**Exercise 3:** In order to play this complete exercise, you *must* start at the tempo at which you can play the sextuplets comfortably.

**Variation 1**

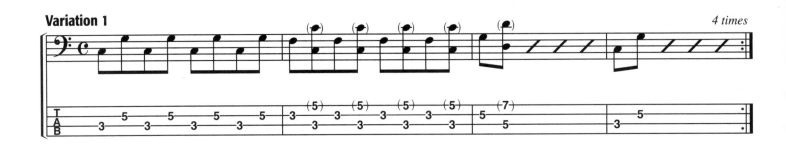

**Variation 2**

**Variation 3**

**Variation 4**

# Unit 3: Advanced Eighth-Note Patterns

Although there is no real substitution for solid eighth-note and sixteenth-note roots in the bass, coming up with original lines to tie these basic rhythms together is both a challenge and an art. Some really great bass-line writers and creators include Jack Bruce, Chris Squire, Paul McCartney, and Tim Bogert, to name just a few. James Jamerson was innovative in both the rhythm and the melodic value of his bass lines. Phil Chen also created some unique lines on all the classic Rod Stewart records. Also check out Noel Redding (Jimi Hendrix), Leon Wilkinson (Lynyrd Skynyrd), and all of the Jethro Tull albums for some great stuff. Transcribing some of these classic bass lines can be extremely helpful. You can analyze them and discover what harmonic and rhythmic devices the artists used when composing their bass lines.

**Exercise 1:** Let's start with this simple bass line over a common chord progression and progressively make it more intricate and, hopefully, more interesting and exciting. We'll use a variety of formulas and techniques.

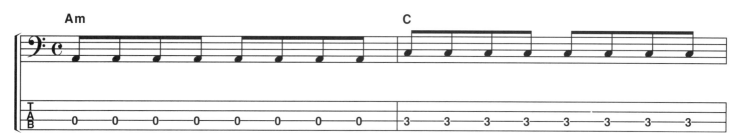

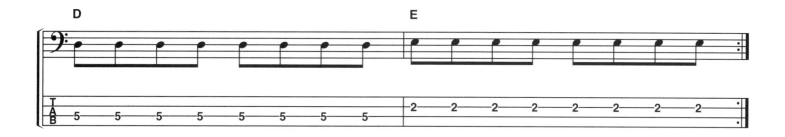

**Exercise 2:** Using scale tones and chord tones creates instant "connections" for these chords. Analyze this line and identify scale and chord tones.

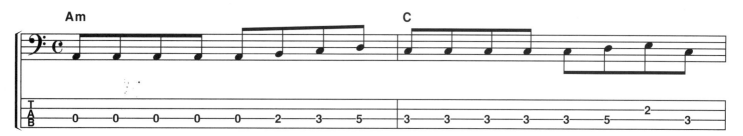

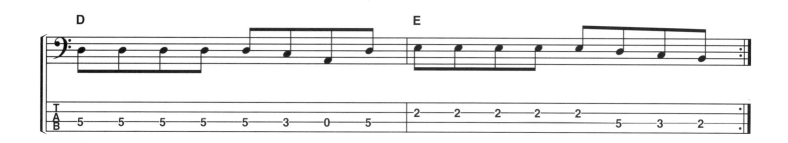

16

**Exercise 3:** Chromatic tones add a little more tension and also make the connection of close chords (chords a whole step or a half step apart) easier. Combining chord tones, scales, and chromatic tones increases your options.

**Exercise 4:** Adding an occasional sixteenth note or some sort of rhythmic variation can enhance the line and make it "tasty." Remember there is a *fine* line between "tasty" and "tasteless." It is extremely easy to overuse these techniques. They are used to enhance the music, not to draw unnecessary attention to the bass line.

**Exercise 5:** Occasionally substituting a 3rd or a 5th for the root can be interesting (such as in the music of Steely Dan, The Police, Yes, etc.). Use the I, IV, V progression as well as the previous example. Exercise 5 shows how it could work.

**Exercise 6:** Analyze the following two lines and identify the components.

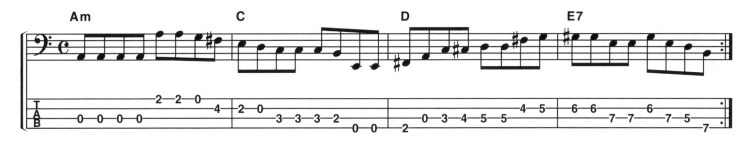

The previous examples are in condensed form. They are designed to give you ideas, and not to be used literally. Experiment with different techniques (chromatic and diatonic scales, rhythmic variations, and harmonic variations) to come up with *your* original lines.

## Technique Builders

**Exercise 7:** You know the routine: start at the sextuplet tempo (this one's a little different).

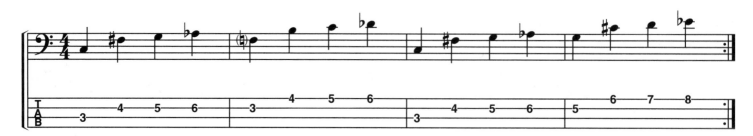

**Var. 1–5:** Use the previous note sequence in the following five variations.

**Variation 1**

**Variation 2**

**Variation 3**

**Variation 4**

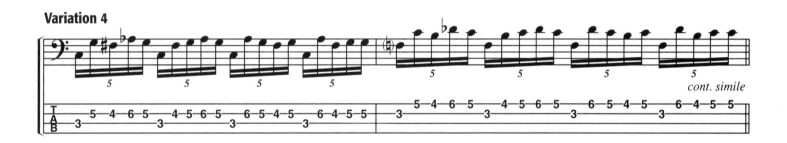

**Variation 5**

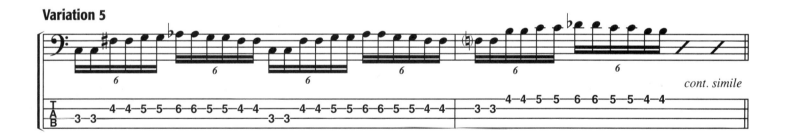

# Unit 4: Technique

**Exercise 1:** Practice this exercise with a metronome. Start slowly, and build up to faster tempos gradually. Your right hand may not cooperate at first—play on your fingertips and avoid superfluous motion.

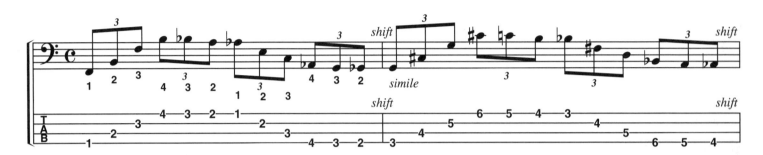

**Exercise 2:** These are variations on the previous exercise. In the first one, you strike every note two times. In the second one, you strike every note three and two times for the odd-meter pattern.

**Exercise 3:** Exercise 3 is followed by four variations. You know the routine: start at the sextuplet tempo (in Variation 4). Repeat each exercise four times. Lay into the quarter notes, grind the eighth notes, and swing the triplets. Also, review units 1 and 2.

**Variations 1–4:** Use the previous note sequence in the following four variations.

**Variation 1**

**Variation 2**

**Variation 3**

**Variation 4**

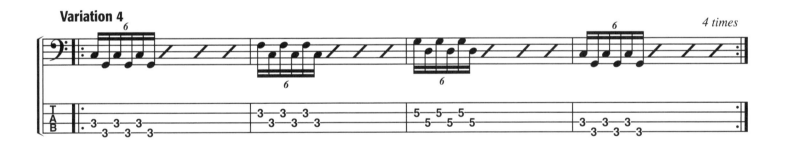

# Lick of the Week

# Unit 5: Bass Lines Utilizing 4ths and 5ths

Until now, we've been dealing exclusively with exercises designed to build technique. The following music examples are actual musical phrases you can use in your playing. From this point forward, "exercises" are for technique building and for reinforcing concepts throughout the neck, in all keys, etc.; "examples" are musical phrases that you can apply to your playing right away.

**Example 1:** Parallel 5ths (ascending) or 4ths (descending) can be a very effective harmonic device, especially when playing in a power trio situation à la Cream, Rush, ZZ Top, etc.

**Example 2:** The 4ths in Example 1 are very similar to a guitarist's power chords. But what happens to the bass line? Ideally, the bass should not suffer due to the chordal movement as shown in this example.

**Exercise 1:** This becomes both a chord study as well as a string-crossing exercise.
Start slow and make it clean (let the upper note sustain as much as possible).

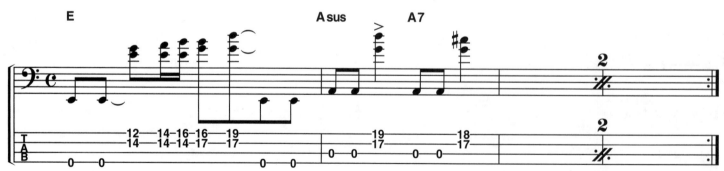

**Example 3:** Adding 3rds (major or minor) further colors the chord. Be careful, because they can muddy the sound (wait until we get to artificial harmonics).

**Example 4:** Three-finger right-hand technique comes in handy at this point, but this example is definitely playable with two fingers.

Use these examples and exercises as a guide to invent your own double-stop passages. Make sure to play them with a group and in time. Stay out of the guitar player's way!

# Technique Builders

**Exercise 2:** The string crossings in this exercise add an extreme level of difficulty. Remember to review previous exercises and examples each week, and always start at a tempo at which you can play the sextuplets comfortably.

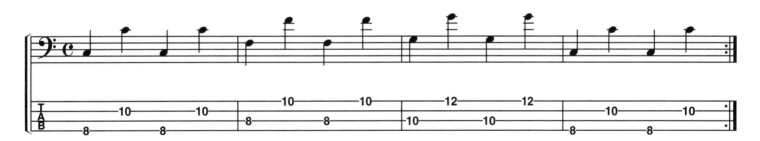

**Variations 1–4:** Use the previous note sequence in the following four variations.

**Variation 1**

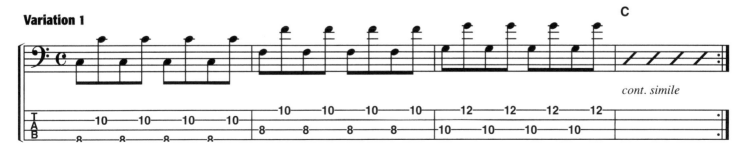

**Variation 2**

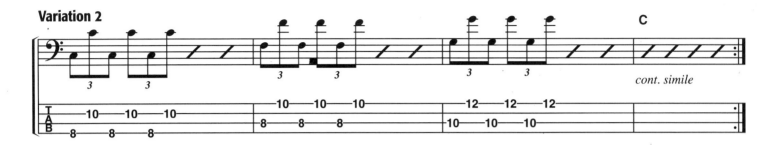

**Variation 3**

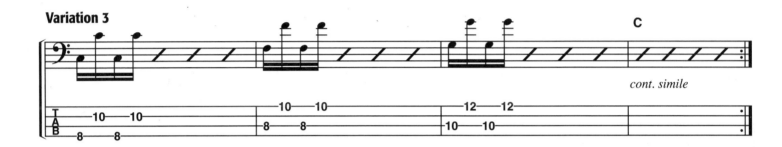

**Variation 4**

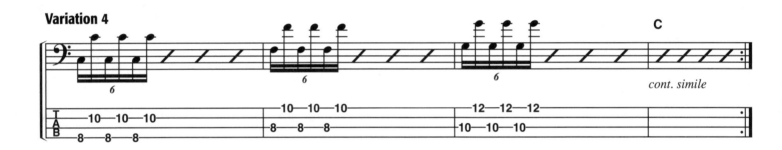

**Examples 5 & 6:** The goal of the following examples is simple: get from one end of the neck up 12 frets as smoothly as possible. Start slowly.

**Example 5**

**Example 6**

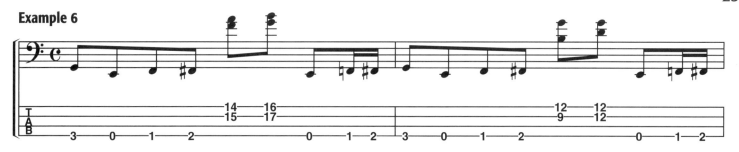

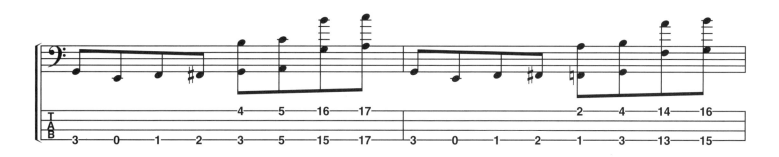

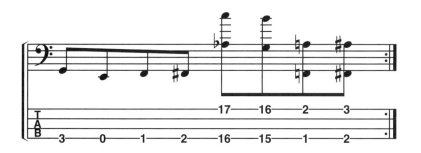

## Lick of the Week

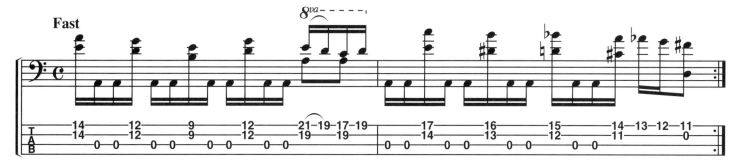

# Unit 6: Finger Busters

**Exercise 1:** Here is a finger buster exercise that is extremely effective for fingering variation, fingerboard knowledge, and position shifting. Some of these fingerings may seem awkward, but they will further your knowledge of extended fingerings and get you out of some scary situations.

**Exercise 2:** As you can see, you start on the G string and smoothly work your way up the neck, crossing strings and shifting to lower strings as you progress. You can see that this is endless. A few more follow. The rule is to take any short motif and transpose it systematically all over the instrument. Keep fingerings consistent and shifts smooth. Leave no fret unturned! (If you follow the fingerings carefully in Example 7, "Mary Had a Little Lamb" could become a challenge.)

**Exercise 3**

**Exercise 4**

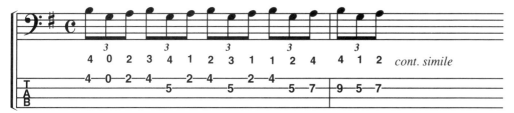

*cont. simile*

**Exercise 5**

*cont. simile*

**Exercise 6**

*cont. simile*

**Exercise 7**

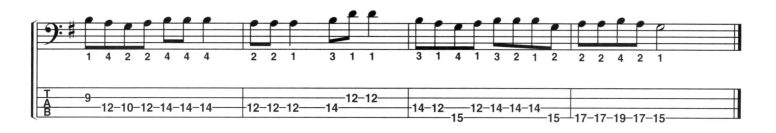

## Single-Position String Crossing

Play this string-crossing example slowly and smoothly, all in one position (you will probably have to stretch or do a "mini-shift" to catch the high notes). Concentrate on right-hand alternation and left-hand accuracy.

# Interval and Left-Hand Exercises

Some fingerings are given as suggestions. Concentrate on making your shifts smooth. Use these exercises
as a guide. Invent your own variations that push your technique to the limit. Think Frank Zappa!

**Example 1**

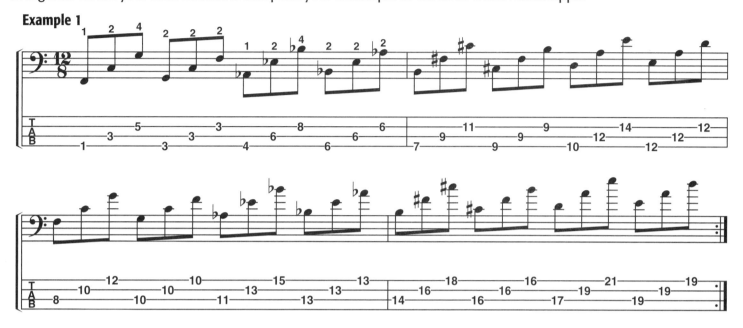

**Example 2**

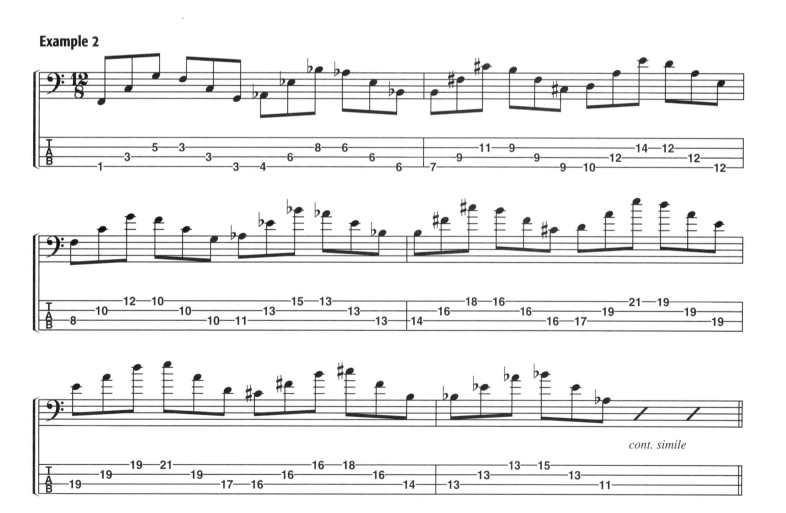

*cont. simile*

# Unit 7: 10ths in Rock (for 4-String Bass)

The use of 10ths and other multiple-stop chord functions can round out or fill up the texture, especially in a power-trio situation (guitar, bass, and drums). They are particularly useful behind guitar solos and melodies, or for creating special effects.

**Example 1**

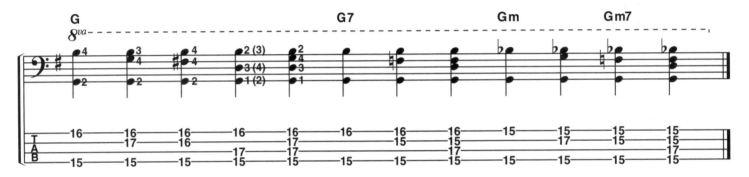

Note: To make multi-stop chords sound cleaner on bass, try moving the notes up an octave or using artificial harmonics (if you know how).

**Example 2: Diatonic 10ths, Major Key**

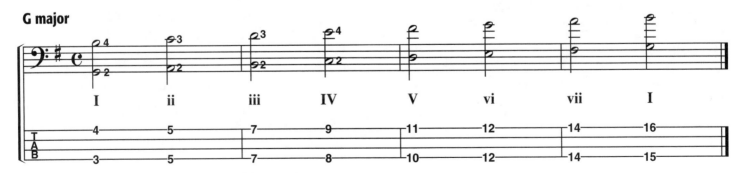

Note: Transpose these examples to different keys.

**Example 3: Diatonic 10ths, Minor Key**

**Example 4**

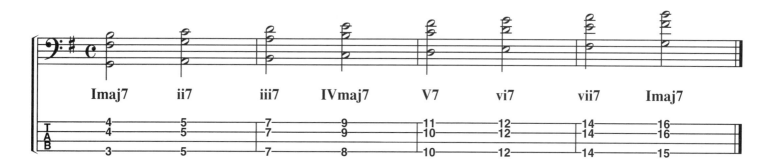

**Example 5**

**Exercise 1:** This exercise is primarily for right-hand development. You can use either two- or three-finger right-hand technique. Combine the different given rhythms to create more complex rhythm patterns (see Example 8).

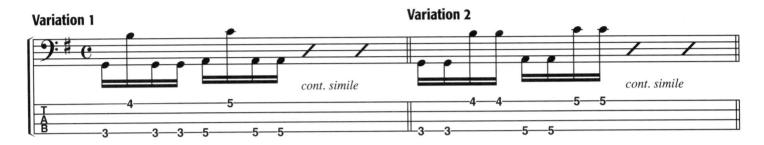

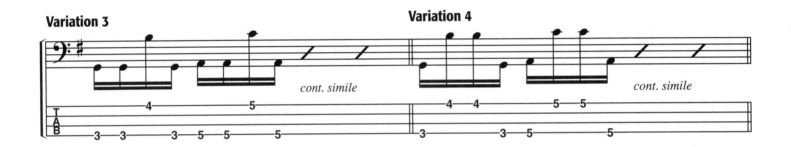

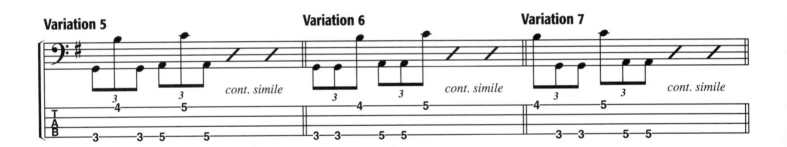

**Exercise 2:** You can add 7ths and 5ths when your technique allows.

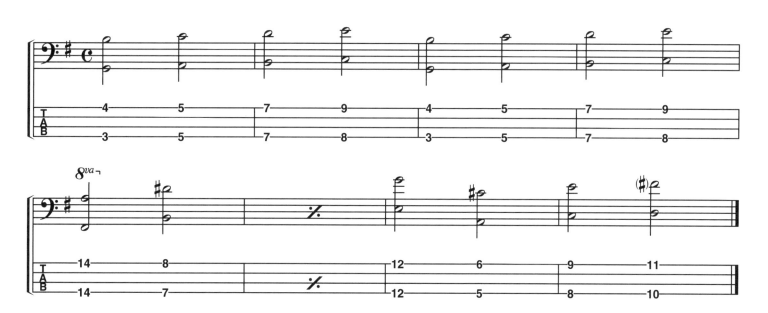

**Slow**

34

## Technique Builders

**Exercise 3:** You know the routine by now! These exercises in 10ths are almost impossible when played using sixteenth notes and sextuplets, but it gives us something to live for. The position shifts are equally as important as the notes themselves. Practice this exercise very slowly until shifts are smooth.

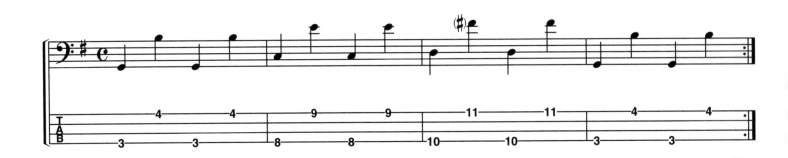

**Variation 1**

**Variation 2**

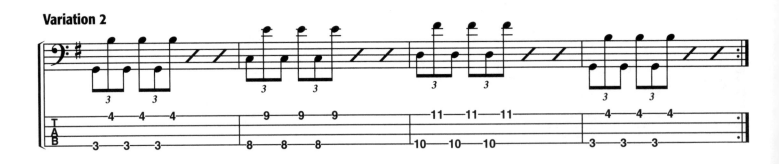

**Variation 3**

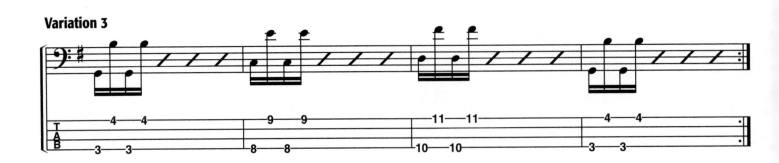

**Variation 4**

*cont. simile*

## Lick of the Week

The sextuplets in this lick are a digital pattern that *can* be played! Make your fingerings logical, especially for the double-stops. You *must* practice with a metronome to develop solid time. This is a good test for your right-hand string-crossing dexterity and left-hand fingering extensions.

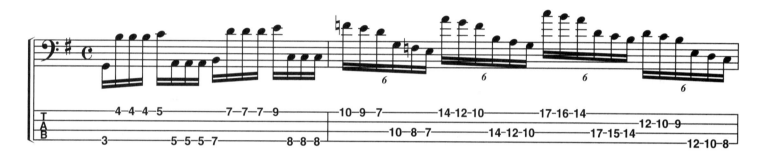

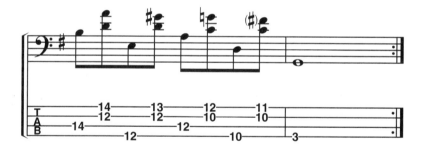

# Unit 8: In the Studio

You finally get the call to record with a big-name act, or your own band is going to do a demo or an album. You spend all day and night getting the parts right and leave feeling good about your playing, only to learn later that the producer called in someone else to overdub your parts. Here are a few tips and good bass lines to keep that from happening. If you have a recording device, record these examples and listen back for an accurate analysis.

**Exercise 1:** Play this exercise using open strings. The notes should ring clearly without any buzzes or noise. If you do get buzzes or noise, you have the following options:

1. Raise the string height (action) of your bass via the bridge string saddles.

2. Have frets filed to an even height.

3. Have your nut re-cut or adjusted.

4. Try a softer attack with your right hand.

5. Try a combination of the above to eliminate the problem.

**Exercise 2:** Play this exercise as you would play it with a band. Listen closely for fret noise on beat 3. Play the pattern from the lowest point to the highest point on your instrument. If you do get a buzz, see the options listed at the top of this page. Sometimes a bent string can also cause buzz. To check for string bends, place the string between your thumb and index finger, then slide upwards rather briskly from lowest to highest. You will feel the bend in the string if it is there.

Note: if you plan on "slapping," do these exercises with your right-hand thumb instead of your fingers, and then adjust your action accordingly.

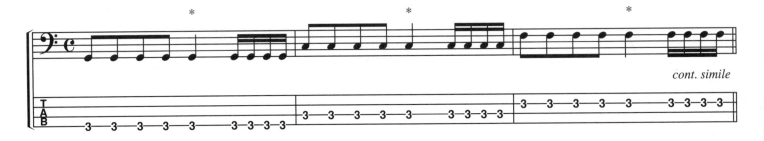

*check for buzz

Make sure your bass' volume sounds even throughout all strings. For example, if your D string volume is weak, raise the pickup or pickup poles under that string. You might have to compensate by dropping the other poles. It is impossible to do this with some bass pickups, so you must adjust string heights to compensate.

# Tips

- If you aren't sure what style of music you will be playing on a session, bring several basses, each with a different tonal quality.

  Your main bass should have fresh strings.

  Your "B" bass could have older strings, especially if the producer wants a classic Motown sound or a less-bright sound (it does happen).

- If fretless is called for, make sure the fretboard is in good condition (no buzzes). To check, plug the bass into the amp, turn up the treble or boost the high (3-8k) frequency (graphic EQ). Play long notes and listen closely. Then, on all strings, play the lowest note (e.g., E♭ on the D string) and slide up rather rapidly. You will hear inconsistencies in the fingerboard as quick zips.

- Know your electronics. If the producer wants a Fender "P-bass" sound and you have a Yamaha bass, know how to get that sound through pickup and tone selection. Every bass is different, but here is a general rule:

      MORE PUNCH = MORE BACK PICKUP

      P-BASS (MORE BOTTOM) = MORE FRONT PICKUP

- You should have one bass with at least two pickups (preferably with active electronics).

- Make sure your batteries are fresh. Have spares.

- Have extra strings.

- Have the necessary tools to make quick string-height and pickup adjustments.

## More Hazard Exercises

**Hazard 2:** You remember the routine for the hazard exercises: keep your finger down after it's through playing. Remember to practice slowly and deliberately, and make your position shifts smooth. If you can't do this hazard smoothly and "honestly," be *patient*; you will get there.

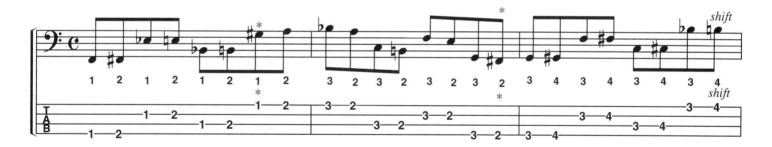

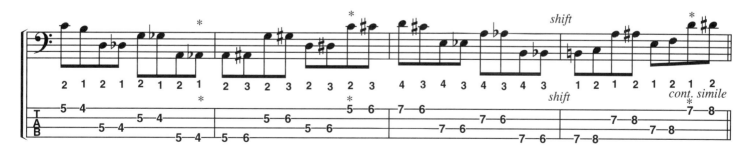

Work towards making it from one end of the fingerboard to the other. When fatigue sets in, stop and rest. If you push for one more bar each day, your goal will be reached within two weeks!

## Movie Theme Excerpt

### by Lou Forestieri
#### (refer to CD)

This is an actual excerpt from a movie theme (used by permission). Sometimes you will be given more (i.e., detailed and written parts) and sometimes less (i.e., nothing). This one has a nice balance.

When creating your own bass lines, strive to fit together with the drum track as well as the mood of the composition.

## Technique Builders

Use of extended fingerings will make this exercise more playable. Standard one-finger-per-fret fingering is very challenging and is shown in parentheses. Concentrate on keeping your right-hand string crossing even.

### Variation 1

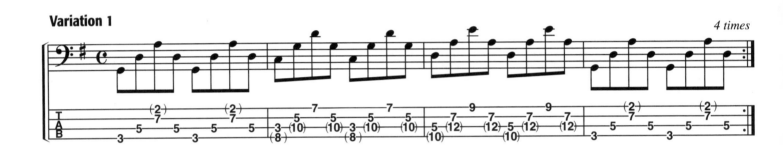

### Variation 2

### Variation 3

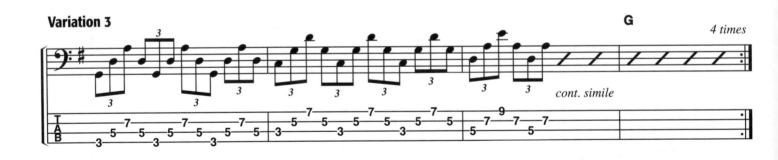

### Variation 4

**Variation 5**

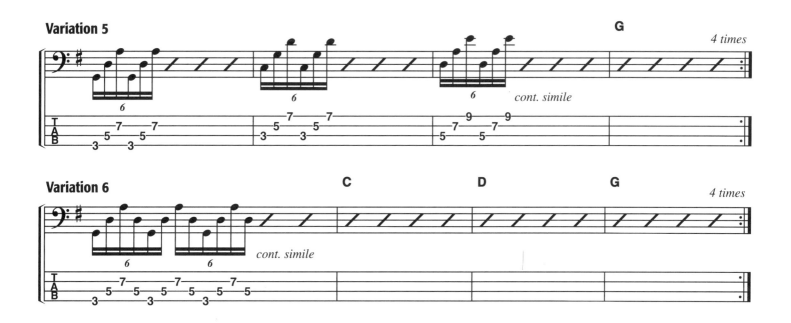

**Variation 6**

# Lick of the Week

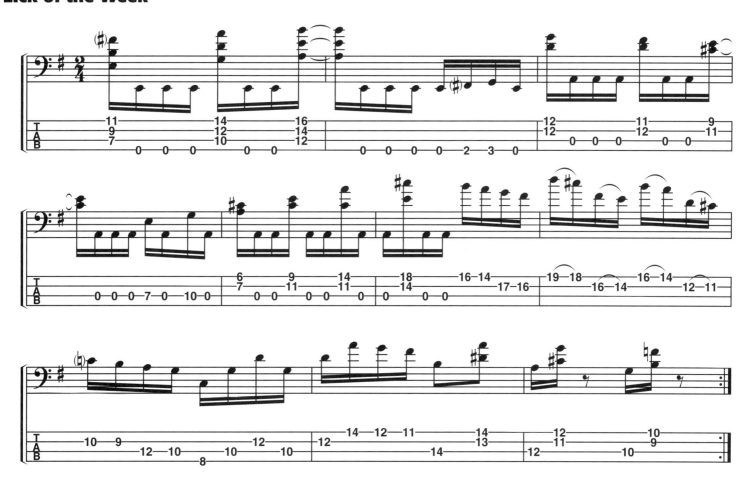

Play this lick slowly. Accuracy and "cleanliness" are the keys to speed.

# Unit 9: Solid-Time Studies

**Exercise 1:** These exercises are designed to solidify your time *feel*. Start slowly and repeat each rhythm several times, eventually tying all of the rhythms together. Try playing this exercise using various note combinations and patterns. Also use different notes and substitute scales!

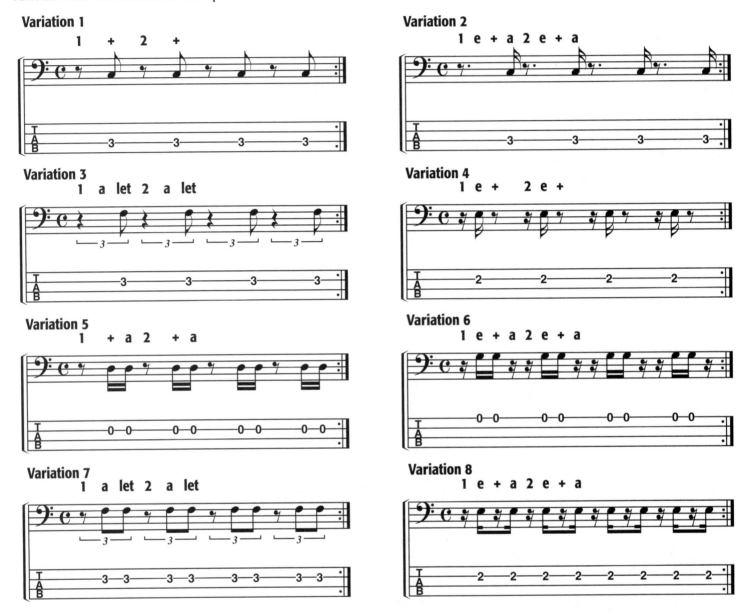

- The metronome is played on every beat.

- Make your notes short and accurate.

- Practice slowly!

**Exercise 2:** Even though it may seem easy, this next exercise is harder! Play quarter notes on every beat, but move the metronome click around to other parts of the beat. You can also invent your own exercise. Do not pass over this exercise without giving it some serious consideration and practice. If this seems easy for you, you're either not playing it right or you've got a really solid time feel!

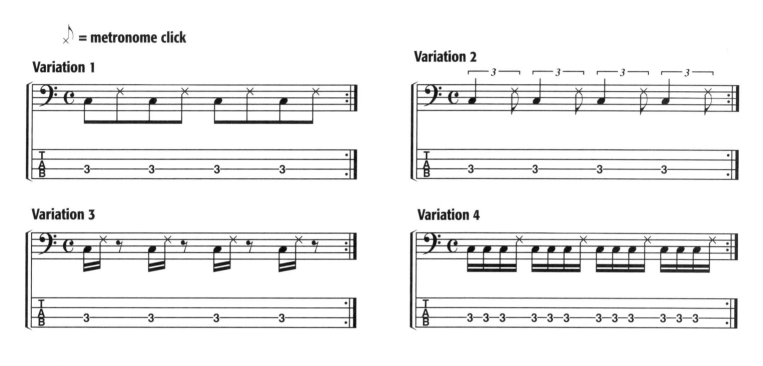

**Exercise 3:** This exercise emphasizes finger discipline by using difficult string-crossing patterns. While not very practical, this exercise helps to discipline your left hand and right hand as well as possibly inspiring you to write some crazy bass lines.

44

## Dexterity Studies

**Exercise 4:** Play this exercise up and down the neck. If you have a 5-string or 6-string bass, play it over the whole instrument. Try to keep your left-hand fingers *low* to the fingerboard and avoid superfluous motion.

## Lick of the Week

Play this lick slowly at first. Concentrate on right-hand finger alternation, left-hand fingering, and smooth string crossing.

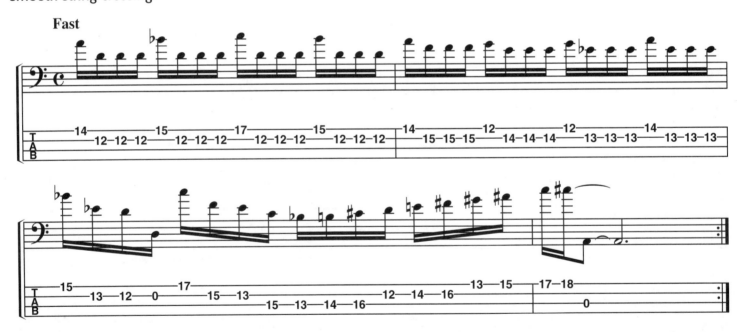

**Exercise 5:** This is an advanced string-crossing exercise with some additional variations. Make up your own (at least two more).

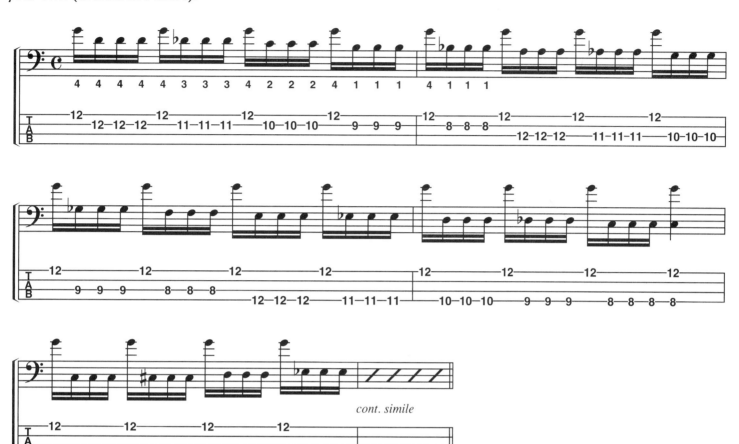

In this exercise, as well as throughout this book, feel free to experiment with other left-hand fingerings.

**Var. 1–4:** Logical left-hand fingerings with extensions are advised in the following four variations.

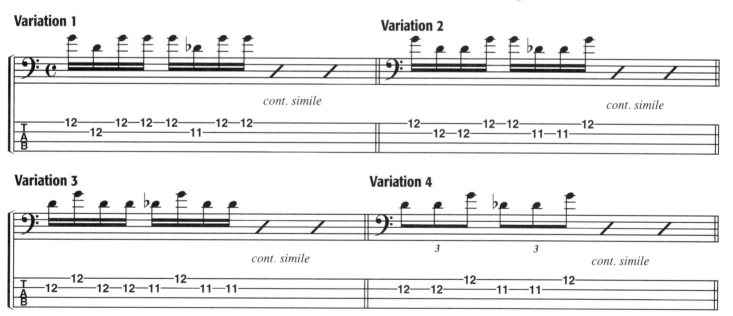

# Technique Builders

**Exercise 6:** You know the routine. Start at the sextuplet tempo.

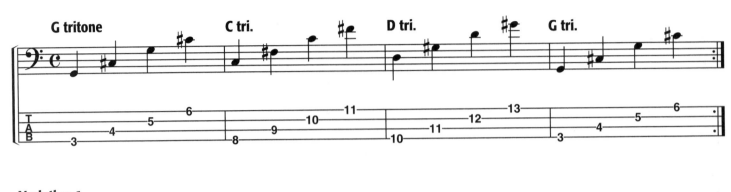

**Variation 1**

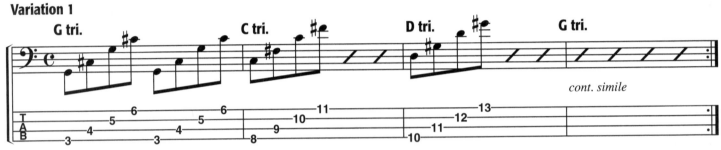

**Variation 2**

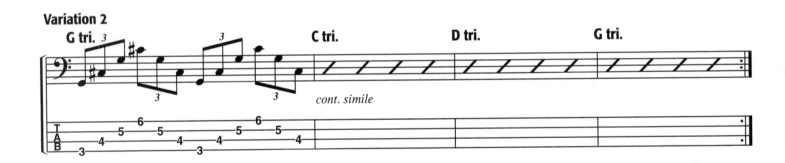

**Variation 3**

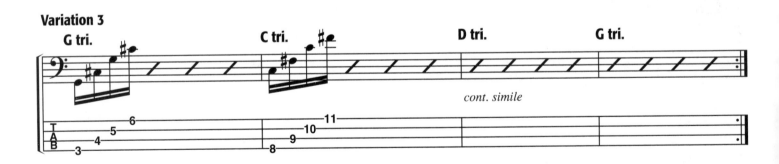

**Variation 4**

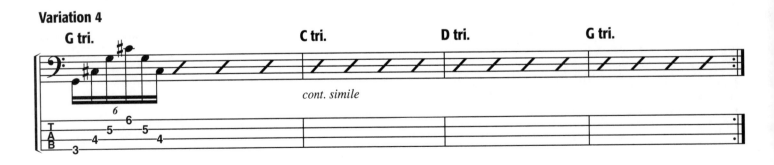

# Unit 10: More Hazard Exercises

**Hazard 3:** These hazard exercises, like the others, should be practiced slowly until you have them under complete control. The most important concept hidden in these exercises is keeping the fingers you've used *stationary*. Your shift is extremely critical. Make it smooth and silent. These exercises are really *difficult*. The substitute bars provided on the next page make them a little easier and can be inserted at the asterisks.

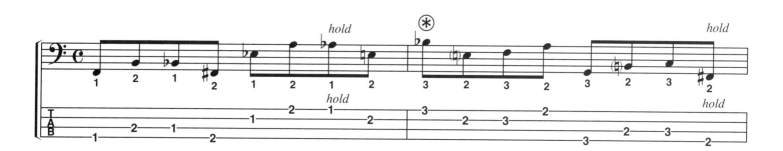

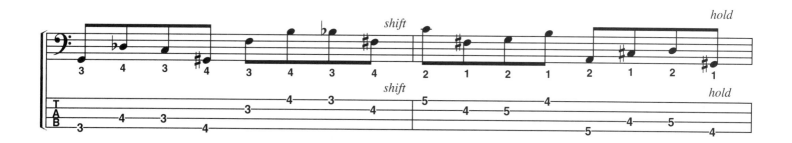

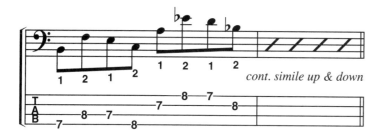

*cont. simile up & down*

## Hazard 4

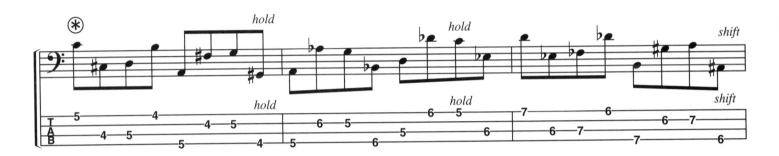

**Substitute Bars:** Your shift is extremely critical. Make it smooth and silent.

48

## Technique Builders

This speed exercise has a new twist to it (downward motion). Try to avoid raking the strings with your right hand. Pick each note, paying attention to your right-hand alternation (slowly). This exercise also places emphasis on parallel 4ths. Try barring the strings with your left hand, and do a light roll to deaden the strings after the attack.

**Variation 1**

**Variation 2**

**Variation 3**

**Variation 4**

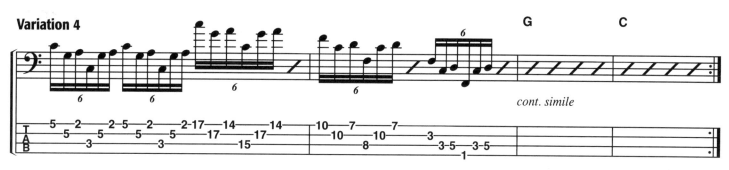

50

## Lick of the Week

This Lick of the Week utilizes some octave displacement as well as triple stops.

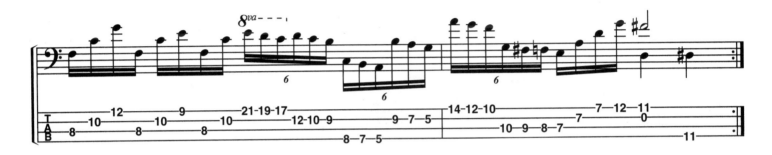

# Unit 11: Odd Groupings

**Exercise 1:** This is an excellent exercise to strengthen your two- or three-finger technique by playing odd-note groups that necessitate starting on a different right-hand finger with each repetition. Make sure that you keep your right-hand finger alternation very consistent. As always, practice these exercises slowly at first. Accent notes where indicated. You can also make up your own patterns using these kinds of groupings. (Right-hand fingering provided for three-finger technique.)

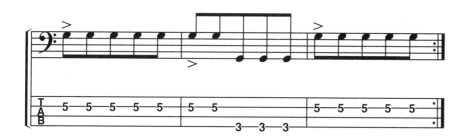

52

**Exercise 2:** This exercise should be repeated many times. Place close attention to the accents. Note the different time signatures.

**Exercise 3:** Remember that these are not strictly odd-time studies. They are designed to develop even right-hand alternation. Practice them very slowly! Make each bar sound identical, even though you are displacing your right-hand finger.

## Technique Builders

**Exercise 4:** Choose your right-hand pattern carefully, and try different combinations to make it work smoothly.

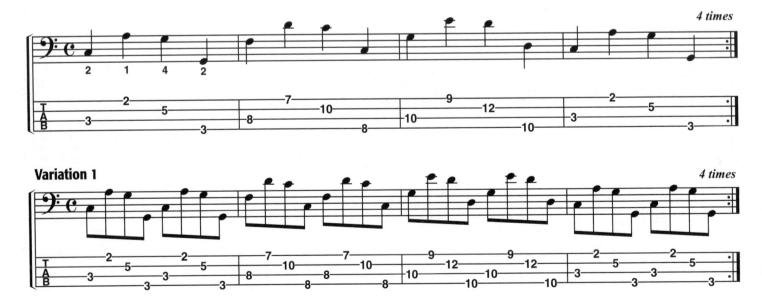

**Variation 2**

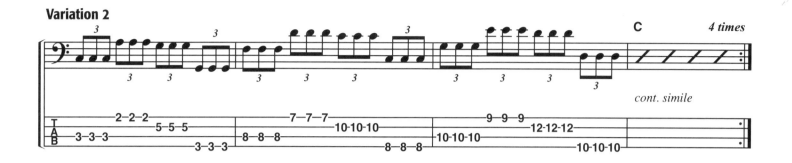

**Variation 3**

**Variation 4**

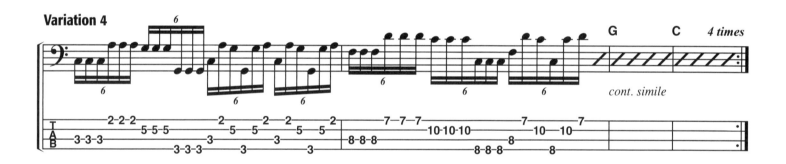

**Variation 5**

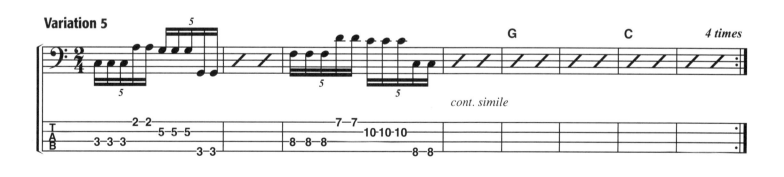

## Lick of the Week

Extended fingerings will really help!

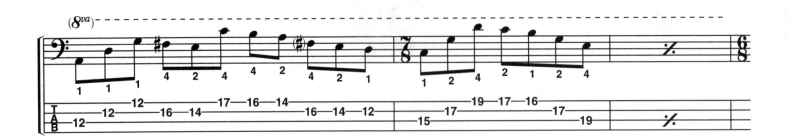

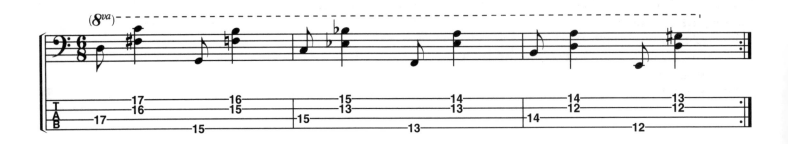

## Conclusion

Read the introduction again. If you can now laugh at it (instead of being scared by it), this book has served its purpose. If it still worries you, start over. Good luck!

Steve Bailey's bass has filled out the low end for a wide range of artists, from Dizzy Gillespie to the Rippingtons, from Jethro Tull to Kitaro, from Willie Nelson to Larry Carlton. He co-founded, with Victor Wooten, the cutting edge all-bass group Bass Extremes. As a faculty member of The Bass Institute of Technology for 10 years and currently Artist in Residence at Coastal Carolina University, Steve has refined, through countless successful students, his approach to teaching bass fundamentals, advanced techniques, and fingerboard mastery. As a sideman, solo artist, educator, and innovator, Steve is known around the world for his mastery of this challenging instrument.